I0472944

The Secrets of Self-Publishing

II

BY THERONE SHELLMAN

ISBN 10: 1475174985
ISBN 13: 978-1475174984

Visit the Author/Publisher:
www.amazon.com/author/theroneshellman

www.facebook.com/theroneshellman
www.twitter.com/theroneshellman
www.blogtalkradio.com/keepingitreal

Editor: English for ARC Book Club, Inc.
Graphics Designer: Mahoganie Underground
Formatted by Anita Davies, for Anita Davies Editing

Table of Contents

Introduction

Therone Shellman as an author and publisher of a small press has experienced every facet of the book publishing world. He's the author of the award winning titles Love Don't Live Here and No Love Lost, co-author of Love.com, author of Survivor I Changed the Rules Part 1(autobiography), and first edition of The Secrets of Self Publishing. All of these titles were published by Third Eye Publishing, a company he established in 2005. The company also went on to publish five other authors. In 2009 Therone had to make the hard decision to release all the authors because of Third Eye Publishing, Inc witnessing distribution issues to the chain retail book store market after its distributor closed its doors.

Therone throughout his literary career has distributed other authors titles to the street market, consulted and has remained a trailblazer and visionary. The Secrets of Self Publishing 2 is an example of Therone's eagerness to learn and also educate.

The Secrets of Self Publishing has helped many authors establish their dreams of becoming self-: published. The Secrets of Self Publishing 2 does not disappoint and starts off where the first edition ended. There are new chapters, and a broader view of the industry is presented. There is even a chapter dedicated to the virtual world of e-book publishing. With the internet age quickly taking over the world, the internet is going to prove to be an important tool to those who want to maintain control of their work and the ability to make a larger profit by cutting spending in the areas of print runs and real world distribution.

The Secrets of Self Publishing 2 is published by Therone Shellman Book Consulting a company Therone Shellman formed to not only take over the publishing of his book titles and branding of his name. But the company also provides consulting services to aspiring authors and established authors as well.

Therone Shellman is available for author interviews and speaking engagements. The fees are very affordable.

1. How to Form Your Company

Literature is covered under the First Amendment of the Constitution of The United States and therefore one has the liberty to sell their books almost anywhere within the territories of the U.S. whether this be in stores or on the streets. There are laws within every county, city, and state that one must adhere to in regard to business enterprises, peddling, and vending. So be mindful of where you are and the laws you need to follow.

Once you package a book and commit to the act of selling it, you're functioning as a business enterprise and *therefore, need to obtain a business license. Whether you form a small business and get a DBA as a* sole proprietor, partnership, LLC, or S Corp the bottom line is most distributors will not consider doing business with you unless you have formed a legitimate business structure. They need to ensure within their business accounting records

11

that authors and publishers' book titles are not being published by their company.

You can go online and access the Small Business Administration (SBA) website to retrieve information and forms, as well as obtain a clear insight into the pros and cons of each business structure.

Visit: www.sba.gov

An accountant, business attorney, and business consultant are also capable of assisting you form your venture and coaching you as to the type of structure that will fit your overall goals.

2. Writing Your Story and Networking with Different Sources

When writing your story you should research and read books in the genre you write in. At the same time, remember to always be unique and write in your own voice. Thousands of books are written and published each year with a limited number of them standing out amongst others within their genre.

So many people wonder and ask the question, "How do you start to write a story?"

"How do you format it?"

For starters, it would be smart to take writing courses because writing and communicating are arts and there is always a better way to express yourself no matter how articulate and gifted you are.

Once your story is written you'll need to have it edited. You can browse online by using search engines and input the words "book editors". It may also be of benefit to visit the sites of online book clubs where other writers hang out to find out who they work with. The Literary Market Place (LMP) and Writers Market (WM) are two resource books that hold a wealth of information in them. In these works you will be able to find a listing of editors and their qualifications. The Writers & Poets and Writer magazines both have classified sections. In here you'll be sure to find several editor service listings.

Every paperback and hard cover book needs a cover or jacket design. Therefore, you're going to need to hire a graphics professional to do the layout. A book cover layout can range anywhere from a few hundred dollars to $1500. Browse through your local bookstore and take a look at the covers of books in your perspective genre to get a good idea of what makes a cover commercially appealing. Remember to always choose a book cover layout that goes along with the book title and overall idea of the story. Many graphics designers are adding their website and company names to the back of the cover. This is an easy way to find someone who is sure to give you the look you're searching for.

Don't forget you'll need an ISBN (international serial book number) in order to have your book stocked in stores. Bowkers is the only firm licensed to create ISBN's in the U.S. Once the ISBN is purchased you will need to have it converted into a barcode. This is the barcode you see on the back cover of books.

You can visit: http://www.bowkers.org

The companies below provide services to covert ISBN's into barcodes.

Visit:
www.simplybarcodes.net and

http://www.barcode-us.com/

Now that you've formed your company, written your story, had it edited, purchased an ISBN, and have a book cover the next step is to get the book printed. From there it must be copyrighted to ensure your rights to the story are protected.

Utilize the internet to download the listing of "101 Best Book Printers".
The Library of Congress website is where you will be able to download copyright forms. Here is where you'll be able to obtain a Library of Congress Catalog Number (LCCN). This is a series of numbers which libraries utilize to catalog a book title and identify it the same way an ISBN identifies a title. The number in many ways resembles an ISBN, but only without the dashes.

3. Distribution

Distribution is probably the most important aspect of publishing. Without distribution you have no way of getting your book(s) inside the hands of readers. It's very simple. You can write as many books as you want but without distribution people outside of your everyday social network will not know who you are.

How you're going to distribute your book(s) is something that should be researched in the very beginning. Again, the LMP and Writers Market will serve as invaluable resource tools. Most Independent Book Distributors who services the chain retail bookstore market also have the capabilities to distribute to "mom and pop" book stores. There are many different markets where you will find your audience.

The internet, book stores, libraries, streets, and neighborhood are only some of the places where you can sell your books.

I've included some of these distributors below:

BCH Fulfillment & Distribution, Diane Musto, President, 46 Purdy Street, Harrison, NY 10528; 914-835-0015; 800-431-1579; Fax: 914-835-0398. Email: bookch@aol.com. Web: http://www.bookch.com

BookMasters Distribution Services, 30 Amberwood Parkway, Ashland OH 44805; 419-281-5100; 800-537-6727; Fax: 419-989-4047. Web: http://www.bookmastersdistribution.com.

Consortium Book Sales, Julie Schaper, President (Sales, Marketing & Publisher Relations) The Keg House, 34 Thirteenth Avenue NE #101, Minneapolis MN 55413-1007; 612-746-2600; 800-283-3572; Fax: 612-746-2606. Email: info@cbsd.com. Web: http://www.cbsd.com.

Greenleaf Book Group, Justin Branch, P O Box 91869, Austin TX 78709; 512-891-6100; 800-932-5420; Fax: 512-891-6150. Email: justin@greenleafbookgroup.com. Web: http://www.greenleafbookgroup.com

Independent Publishers Group, Mark Suchomel, President, 814 N Franklin Avenue, Chicago IL 60610-3109; 312-337-0747, ext. 209; 800-888-4741; Fax: 312-337-1807. Email: suchomel@ipgbook.com. Web: http://www.ipgbook.com

Ingram Publisher Services, One Ingram Boulevard, P O Box 3006, La Vergne TN 37086-1986; 615-213-5349; 800-937-8100; Fax: 615-213-5597.
Email: Publisher@ingrampublisherservices.com.
Web: http://www.ingrampublisherservices.com
National Book Network, Ginger Miller, 4501 Forbes Boulevard #200, Lanham MD 20706; 301-459-3366, ext. 5510; Fax: 301-429-5746.
Email: gmiller@nbnbooks.com.
Web: http://www.nbnbooks.com

Take the time to research the distributors above. Remember, there are a whole lot more independent distributors out there so get on the internet and do your research. I've started the search for you. The secrets of self-publishing are the same as the secrets to success. One must be willing to research all outlets, and find a method which fits your program. There is no one written rule. Mainstream distributors' payment arrangements vary. Most companies usually pay the author or publisher for the sales six months after the title releases, and every six months thereafter. This is not always the case, so be sure to check with the distributor.

Guerilla Marketing is an area that all independent authors and publishing companies should come to know and it falls within the scope of marketing and distribution. This is basically obtaining book sales outside of the normal distribution channels. For instance, street or neighborhood book signings, book sales to street vendors or local bookstores and gift shops are good examples of guerilla marketing.

20

African American authors and independent publishers have access to a small number of distributors that cater to their works. I've compiled a list of some. I must add that these are not the only ones. New distributors are springing up here and there as more entrepreneurs see the need to provide these services.

Black Book Plus/ Seaburn Book Distributors: 33-18 Broadway; Astoria, N.Y. 11106
(718)267-2679

African World Books: 2217 Pennsylvania Ave.; P.O. Box 16447; Baltimore, MD 21217
(410) 383-2006

The African American Independent Distributors mentioned above in most cases commence payments on book sales ninety days after they stock a title, or the title releases.

3A. Distribution: Work the system: Don't Let the System Work You.

Without distribution and the means of getting your books to the public you will have very little success. Do an internet search by keying in "Top Independent Book Distributors". Research the companies thoroughly to obtain a clear idea as to the types of books they distribute and the markets they deal with. For the author who has written their first title and who more than likely will have a hard time obtaining distribution for their work through one of the large distributors, it is recommended that you visit the Baker & Taylors website: http://www.btol.com

Through their publisher partnership program, independent authors and publishers are able to market their titles to the libraries and get their titles into the chain retail bookstores. In order for chain retail stores and most libraries to stock an independent title the books must be distributed by an acceptable distributor or wholesaler.

Unlike some independent bookstores, Barnes and Noble will not order books straight from the publisher. Barnes and Noble does have an Acquisitions Department, which reviews new titles by independent publishers, but even if they do place an order they will not, in most cases, order more than 40-100 books. And they make a practice of ordering from the publishers' distributor.

Applications can be downloaded from the website: http://www.barnesandnoble.com

As you grow look for ways to develop and nurture your own ability to control some of your distribution. Remember the system is designed for you to fail because; everyone from the wholesaler to the bookstore is in your pocket and eating away at your profit. Sell your books door to door, on the streets, and in the churches. Get them everywhere you can so you can see more of your money, but at the same time utilize the system. In between distributor payments, this will allow you to have a steady flow of cash.

Even if you have a distributor, you should not depend on them solely to sell your books. Regardless of how you start out you should always seek to maximize your sales and exposure by implementing a sales program where you also sell your book(s). Pack your books in your trunk and hit the local shopping centers and areas where there are a lot of people. This is a great way to build buzz about your work while you build capital.

Beware that as you grow from title to title you create a budget for projects because as with money, book sales also come in spurts. Meaning one month you may sell a ton of books and then the next month you may sell a small fraction of what you sold the previous month. You may find yourself paying for upcoming projects that will not release months down the line but you're not currently selling that many books or receiving book sale payments. This is what happens to most publishers who expand too quickly. So be careful and crawl before you walk. It's probably a good idea to sit down with an established publishing professional or a business consultant that is knowledgeable about business growth, financing etc.

Visit the Small Business Administration site: www.sba.gov

There is also a division called The Service Core of Retired Executives. These mentors provide free online and face-to-face mentoring and business counseling to those who are looking to start a business or those who are in business already.

The Service Corp of Retired Executives site: www.score.org

From personal experience, I will tell you that distribution is one of the most important aspects of publishing. Once it's established if you lose it, or it's disrupted your business will definitely be affected in a negative way.

3B. How to Distribute Your Own Books

One of the best ways a self-published author or small press can kick off the start of their own distribution program is to start with an individual author, or small press website. The website should detail information about the author(s), company, book covers, synopsis(s), and links either to PayPal or other merchant accounts where payments are transferred to your bank account.

You may also choose to establish an Advantage account with Amazon.com, stock books with them, and have the payment link on your website linked to Amazons item page. Therefore the customer buys off the Amazon site after being transferred from your site. Amazon makes payments directly to you by depositing payments electronically into your bank account.

An author or publisher should always exploit ways to sell a percentage of their own titles to customers, vendors, booksellers, and "mom and pop" stores. It's as simple as direct sales, or giving books on consignment to booksellers (vendors). The objective of direct distribution is a quick return on investment so it's imperative to watch your cash flow. It's in your best interest to ensure that not too many of your books are in the hands of sellers if payments aren't being received. The quicker you get return on your investment the quicker you can reinvest the profits. With all this said if you're not a good seller you should then hire someone who is.

Book vendors who set up on the streets and inside locations are invaluable contacts, for their inventory usually ranges from 50 to a few hundred different titles. The books are usually turned over quickly and therefore authors and publishers receive payments a lot quicker than dealing with normal distributors.

It's the ideal desire of every independent author and publisher to distribute their own title(s) instead of having to deal with a distributor. There are instances where authors and publishers with ten or more titles can arrange a distribution relationship with Ingram Wholesalers directly. This may be a sure way for any author who is wary about dealing with distributors mismanaging their titles to get their books into the chain.

3C. When a Distribution Agreement Goes Wrong

The Pros of dealing with a mainstream distributor is that it's not just you alone vying for team bookshelf space in bookstores for your books. You now also have a company with staffed sales who are also working for you. Within most cases, these sales reps who work for the distributor receive a commission from the book sales they make. This in essence means their earnings and livelihood depend on them doing their jobs. This is to conduct sales.

The downside of dealing with a mainstream distributor is that most terms are exclusive. This means they are the only distributor that can service the markets covered in the contract. This can be both a good and bad thing. If they are a strong company with talented and competent sales reps then you are in the best possible business situation in regards to publisher/distributor relations. However, if they are a company that mismanages funds, run by a poor management team, and the sales reps do not know how to represent the broad range of titles distributed by the company you are then soon to be in a lot of trouble. Even if the company isn't run into the ground you are basically in the same situation as if it had.

Of course, there is always a provision that states either party has the right to dissolve the business relationship in writing within a certain amount of days. Notice is usually to be served 30-45 days before requested termination is to take place.
Always have in mind that whatever copies of books the distributor has sold they can possibly withhold a percentage of pay from you in case of possible bookstore returns. Dissolving a distributor relationship can get very messy. So it's very necessary to have your paperwork and accounting in order so you can evaluate the total scope of the situation.

For damage control, you should always ensure that any distributor agreement you sign also has information in regards to how you can go about resolving issues you have, such as a department or individual contact within the company where you can have an issue resolved. There should also be an ability to take the matter to arbitration if this individual cannot resolve the issue. For your own insurance never sign a distribution agreement which doesn't possess the above provisions.

One of the best ways to know where you stand as far as business terms in regards to the distributor is to constantly stay in contact with the representative assigned to your company. If you witness them not being responsive to you and your needs, request to speak to someone on the next level. At this point, state your concerns, and request a new representative to represent your company's titles.

The more you're on top of your business the easier it will be for you to reap the benefits of good relationships.

4. Composing an E-Book and Digital Distribution

Since the emergence of eBooks publishers have been scrambling to cash in on a market which has quickly become 10% of the retail book sales market. Online and chain retail bookstores have eBook conversions and in some cases their own eBook readers. Amazon has an eBook reader called the Kindle, Barnes and Noble has the Nook eBook reader.

If you would like to sell your book titles on Amazon.com, you can create an author/publisher Kindle account. You will have to upload a MS Word file document of the manuscript and the converter will compile and format the document for you. This is fairly easy. You will then have to fill in all the information like price, company name, author, etc. You will also be able to upload the book cover. With

Barnes and Noble you will have to utilize the contact form to let them know you would like to have your title available in eBook form for the Nook. Sony eBook Reader and Apple iPad are other eBook readers that are quickly gaining popularity. Pretty soon there will be dozens of these devices competing for eBook revenue. According to Amazon.com, eBook sales rose 193 percent in 2010 from 2009. International Digital Publishing Forum collects quarterly US trade retail eBook sales in conjunction with the Association of American Publishers. Their statistics state the third quarter of 2010 eBook sales totaled $119.7 million.

If you would like to create your own eBooks to distribute from your author/publisher websites there are plenty of software programs on the market to assist you with this task. Below I will list a few:

EPaperFlip.com/Dynamic

www.3DIssue.com

www.ebookscompiler.com

Publishers state that paperback and hard cover books aren't going anywhere anytime soon. Yet, they aren't ignoring the fact that the book buying community is quickly going tech. One thing is for sure - eBook sales are bound to keep climbing as the year's progress. As an independent author you should be cashing in on this great opportunity. For starters, self- publishers will save on book printing costs. After the initial costs of editing, purchasing an ISBN, book cover, and marketing the rest is all earnings. If you deal with Amazon.com via Kindle or barnesandnoble.com via the Nook, unlike dealing with physical books, you will not have lengthy distribution agreements. It's a win/win for the author/publisher and online retailer and you get to sell the produce over and over without having to reinvest profits earned. You cannot get any better than this!

5. Marketing & Publicity

Marketing and Publicity are two very misunderstood terms by publishing newcomers and because of this, even books published with sound distribution programs fail unnecessarily.

There are two types of marketing. One is inbound and the other is outbound.

Inbound marketing is knowing your product and potential customers and how your product meets their needs.
*The pricing of your product and packaging as well as whom your competitors are.
*Branding the product so it has a personality that is different from your competitors'.

Outbound marketing is advertising and marketing, sales and publicity focused on your Organization. It also includes customer service.

Most of the time writers/ publishers focus solely on outbound marketing. As a result they strive to push their books onto people and organizations, which really aren't interested. Effective inbound marketing often produces more effective outbound marketing and sales.

Publicity is about getting information to the media in order to capture a larger audience. The public, the radio and TV are examples of publicity outlets. Many times marketing gets confused with publicity. In fact, some book marketers call themselves publicists when all they do is set up book signings, write press releases and organize book club discussions. Publicity on the other hand primarily deals with the media. So before you start kicking out big bucks for a publicist, make sure the individual or company has the ability to get you mass exposure. Some marketing resources for authors and independent publishers:

Book Marketing
http://www.bookmarket.com

BookSense
www.bookweb.org/booksense/publisher/publisher/3311.html

Library Market Place

www.literarymarketplace.com/lmp/us/resources.asp
/

PMA

www.pma-online.org

SPAN

www.SpanNet.org

Aside from distribution, marketing and publicity are the next important elements and aspects of publishing. Heavy online marketing helped propel my book signings to 20-50 book sales at the chain retail book stores, and street signings. Within two plus years, I garnished 16,000 book sales of the title. About 5,000 of them were through the bookstores. I admit MySpace at the start of my career was the best thing that ever happened to me.

5A. Book Marketing: Where to Spend Your Money and Time

Like in any other business everyone wants your money! And everyone has to make a living. If writing is how you make your living or part of your income then your job is to put your money, as far as marketing your title is concerned, in markets where you're going to obtain book sales or exposure for you and your title. I say exposure because, depending on what your title is about it may open doors to other opportunities. For instance, because of my title "Love Don't Live Here" and the story background consisting of an issue considered by some to be of social importance, I've been able to speak at schools, institutions and do feature articles in magazines in print via online. And in some cases I've been paid a fee to do so.

If your title is a non-fiction book that entails political science as the subject matter, it wouldn't make sense to market your book on an online site that mostly hosts contemporary fiction. The best thing to do is stay within the boundaries of your titles genre. You want to be where the prospective readers of your genre go plain and simple.

There are those cases where it is good to separate yourself from the crowd and place your books in markets where there may be no other books sold. For instance, specialty stores in your neighborhood. I have sold many books this way. Wherever I see vendors selling clothing, CDs, etc. I always ask them if they would like to sell some of my books as well.

Magazines are another good venue no matter what genre you are in. If you write chic lit or woman fiction then it would be a good idea to strive to get articles in women magazines. It's not hard at all to do, especially if you are willing to provide ideas and input for the article so that most of the work is done by you. This is cost effective free advertising as well, which might of cost you $300-$800 to place an ad in this same magazine depending on the add space. And unlike online interviews or chats, magazines stay around and get passed around as long as people find the information in them useful.

Sit in with book clubs, online Q&A interviews and online phone interviews present the ability for you to reach a few dozen to thousands of potential readers.

If you are self-published, always keep books and promotional items on you or around you at all times. Also, make sure that you obtain a website done by someone who is experienced with designing professional websites. Someone who can incorporate all the things you need to maximize your products exposure on the web.

5B. Helpful Marketing Guides and Literary Resources for Self-Publishers

Whether you are an aspiring author, self published or signed the following books are invaluable resource tools:

*The Self Publishing Manual: Dan Poytner

*Complete guide to Self Publishing: Tom Ross, Marilyn Ross

*1001 Ways to Market your books For Authors and Publishers: John Kremer

*Complete Guide to Book Publicity: Jodee Blanco

*Guerilla Marketing for Writers: 100 Weapons to Help You Sell Your Work: Jay Conrad Levinson

*Unlocking the Secrets of Independent Publishing: Sylvia Hemmerly

If you are looking for a literary professional, such as an editor, publicist, literary agent or a publishing

house to submit your manuscript to I recommend that you pick up these two resource books:
*Writers Market: Kathryn S. Brogan
*LMP (Literary Market Place): Information Today Inc.

There are plenty of literary publications but here are just a few of the most notable. The two I subscribe to are at the top:
*The Writer: www.writermag.com
*Poets & Writers: www.pw.org/mag
*Foreword Magazine: www.forewordmagazine.com
*Library   Journal:
www.libraryjournal.reviewsnews.com
*Black   Issues   Book   Review:
www.bibookreview.com

If you need to send out press releases I recommend the following service providers:
*PRWeb.com
*www.PR.com
*www.blackpr.com

5C. Guerilla Marketing beyond the Store for Independent Authors &Small Presses

Below are some pointers on how to market your work beyond the store market.

*Street book signings with and without street vendors. Strive to also work it out for them to carry your title(s).

*Seek to get your title(s) in "mom and pop" specialty stores where they sell DVD's, CD's etc. Your book stands a better chance where there are not hundreds of other books.

*Create postcards which have all of your titles info as well as where they can buy the books at online and off. Ensure that the vendors who carry your book(s) also have copies. Whether it's a sale now or a sale six months later it's still a sale.

Promotional materials allow customers the opportunity to order later on.

*Write magazine and newspaper articles. Strive to put your name out there as much as possible. With each article always sign off leaving info on how to contact you on the net, your personal or company website address etc. it's not hard to reach out to magazines online and off and there are so many which are always looking for writers with fresh ideas. The internet makes it a lot easier to reach the key people you need to get in contact with.

*Always speak about what you do and what your stories and work are about, whether it's at a signing or just a person you are meeting in the street. I've acquired a few speaking engagements at universities and organization functions because my stories all revolve around social issues. And because, I'm so vocal about my political and social views, I get invited to events which most fiction authors don't. The bottom line is being vocal leads to exposure.

*Promote and help others. Whether it's a book blurb and seeing your name in print or just a point in the right direction and having this person speak your name. The bottom line is its promotion.

*Use the internet and writer blogs to reach an audience that you may never see in person. Your views are a representation of who you are, so whenever possible speak about your writings, etc.

6. Understanding Expense and Profit Margin

Creating a budget for your book is no different than creating a business plan for a business. Since your book is your business, the budgeting plan will serve as a key part of your overall business plan

In creating your budget the following elements should be included: editing, typesetting of manuscript, ISBN, graphics designer for book cover, book print run, author/company website, press-kit, and author head shot photos, press release distribution services, online marketing, online advertising, possible marketer or publicist services. Possible distribution channels as well. The above may seem a bit overwhelming but a well-rounded budget will help piece together a comprehensive publishing program. Too many times authors/publishers under fund a book title and as a result, sales and profit fall below expectations and possibilities.

Below is an example of a sample budget plan. All of this is assuming you've already set up your business as a sole proprietorship, LLC, or S-Corp.

360 page double spaced manuscript

Editing: $2.50 per page x 360 = $900
Typesetting of manuscript $200
Isbn $125
Author/company website $500
Press-kit $450
Business cards/post cards $300
Press-release distribution (2 websites) $250
Online marketing (2-4 websites) $400-$1000
Book cover design $550
Final typeset of manuscript 280 pages
Print run for 1,500 copies of book $2, 835
1500/ $2,835.00= $1.89 per book

The above is just an example blue print to go by. These are not actual numbers in regards to money amounts.

Total= $6,510-$7,110

The above is a very simple outline. But one will be surprised at how many self-published authors actually don't create a budget for their projects. In return, they wind up putting their project out in a crazed state. They either under spend or over spend.

Hold on I'm not finished!
Now that we see you'll have to spend $6,510-$7,110 to fund your project, let's look at your break-even point. This is the point at which you recoup the money you invested.

If your book is priced retail at $14.95 and you provide 600 copies to distributors at 60% off retail ($5.98 a copy) then set aside 300 copies for yourself to sell at $10.00 a copy. Provide 600 copies to vendors, and non-traditional store locations at $7.00 a copy a copy. Let's see the Total.

Distributor 600 copies x $5.98 = $3,588
Personal sales 300 copies x $10= $3,000
Vendors, nontraditional store locations 600 copies x $7.00= $4,200

Total= $10,788

From the figures above, it shows that from the first print run of 1,500 books the initial investment will be recouped. In addition, there will be a profit to reinvest.

It's imperative that when starting out one has the ability to keep business funds separate from living expenses. As the figures show if one is able to do this, then upon the first print run one will be able to establish a solid foundation from which to build a career and business. More important than money is the ability to manage finances.

7. Negotiating a Publishing Contract

Most large traditional publishing companies request that an author is represented by a literary agent. The agent in-turn will submit the work to the publisher for review. Publishing companies who operate under this standard will not under any circumstances review work from a perspective author.

Independent publishing companies on the other hand, in most cases, allow authors to submit their own work(s) to be reviewed. For the author who is too busy to handle the behind the scene work that comes with publishing, this option may be the best. The author can concentrate on writing and building a readership while the publishing company can worry about bookstore shelf space, and getting the work to sellers online and off.

Publishing company contracts vary. An author can expect to either be paid a flat sum for their work, or receive royalties from each book sale. In regards to royalties the common industry rates for paperback titles in the independent market is 7.5-11%, and hardcover is 9-10%.

The usual question asked by new authors in regards to having their work put out by a publishing company is whether or not they are responsible for the marketing of their books. The answer is it's the authors' job to market their work and develop their readership. Some publishers do assist in this process but generally, they aren't obligated to.

In regards to seeking a publishing contract from one of the large publishing houses; for the self-published author who has developed a following this means you have more negotiating power and leverage than aspiring authors. This is the author who has never been published. Publishing is a business, and publishing contracts are designed for the publisher to make money. Therefore, an author should approach the business of having their work published with the same mind state as the publisher who is in business mode. Business is business, so don't feel out of place to negotiate terms that allow you to seek more profits from the sale of your work.

Before signing any agreement you should always seek counsel; preferably legal counsel. However, an established author or literary professional can also explain to you the language of the contract and all it entails.

Always review the complete contract from start to finish. Don't leave anything to chance. If there is any single word you don't understand, or any sentence seek out a publishing professional who can shed some clarity on whatever confuses you.

After your book is taken on by a publisher to be published this begins the real work. It's no longer good enough to write an excellent book for it to sell. Marketing is the fuel behind what sells books in this time and age in the publishing world.

Since marketing is the key to book sales, the minute you come to terms with what type of book you want to write you should also be coming to terms with how you plan to market the book. Whether your intentions are to self-publish or seek out a publisher, the end result is that it's the author's responsibility to market their own work.

Having your work published by a publishing company can be a benefit because you will not have to focus on the complications of running a publishing company. Instead, you can put all of your focus into writing, marketing and building your readership.

8. Record Keeping and Budgeting

In order to be successful in any business it's necessary to be organized and on top of your business. Therefore, record keeping and budgeting will be one of the most important key factors in determining whether a business fails or flourishes. Keeping good business records will help you increase profit and point out areas that need to be worked out.

QuickBooks Pro by Intuit is a software product that I currently utilize. You can print checks, pay bills, track expenses, send invoices, download card and bank transactions, organize data, track sales, create profit and loss statements and do much more. The company's phone number is (888)729-1996.

QuickBooks is not the only business budgeting software on the market, and there are so many other good products. Do an online search under "business software" and a listing will come up of companies and products.

There is also software made specifically for publishers, which can accomplish invoicing, payments, returns, inventory, customer contacts, royalties, and so much more. Below I will list some of the companies out of the many who provide software specifically for the needs of publishers.

DashBook Version 1: www.DaskBook.com

Business System for Publishers: www.ipub.com

Publisher Manager: www.trilogyusa.net

9. The Pros and Cons of Book Signings March 28, 2007 Book Section Myspace Feature

Below is not the complete article that MySpace featured of my work. I edited and condensed it to fit the needs of this project.

Book signings technically are meant for promotional purposes. Fortunately, I've been able to garnish sales out of them as well. But most authors are introverts and others aren't aggressive enough or out-going enough so book signings may not be a good medium to look for sales.

There are many things to consider like traveling expenses, time and whether or not store patrons will be able to come back and purchase your title at the store once you leave. For starters if the store does not carry your book and it is out of the way of where you live and reside, then it is not a good idea to do a book signing at this store location. In these cases stick to stores who do carry your title(s). It is important to weigh in and consider all the factors before setting up an extensive book tour which extends beyond your state.

It's also important to develop sales leads for future titles, so when you do book signings make sure you bring a notebook or pad to take email addresses of people who purchase your title. For my first title "Love Don't Live Here" I started a little late but I still managed to obtain over 2,500 email addresses.

Time is everything and there is not enough of it to waste in a day! For authors, self-publishers and small publishers it's so important to utilize your time wisely on people and areas that will enable you to grow and expand your sales. You can pull your car up into a local shopping center, salon, barbershop, etc. and sell just as many books if not more than you will by going to a store out of your state area. If this store does not carry your books then after you leave the store you will not garnish any book sales. The end result will be a big negative. In fact, by going to a local shopping center you didn't have to pay tolls or gas.

9A. Protocol for Setting up Book Signings

Time factor for setting up a book signing should be no less than six weeks in advance. This way the store will be able to order the books from the wholesaler, distributor, and you will be able to send bookmarks and promotional material weeks in advance of the signing.

Obtain the name and phone number of the store manager, and events coordinator. In the process let them know that you will be calling them back in two weeks. Also, leave a contact number so they can call you if anything arises.

4 weeks before the signing make a follow up call to make sure the books were ordered. Again, make sure that the stores contact person has either your number or your publicists' number.

2 weeks before the date, call to make sure the books have arrived.

Always strive to show up at a book signing at least 45 minutes early, so that you can set up and canvass the area to hand promotional material to store patrons, and possibly browse the surrounding area of stores to make contact with people to possibly attend your signing.

For presentation it is good to have a large billboard/poster and easel if possible. Be courteous, dressed neatly and wide awake. If you're having a bad day then pretend that you are having the best day of your life because it is you who people buy before they even take an interest in purchasing your book.
The rest is a hustle!

9B. Selling Books in the Street Market

The street market provides the possibility of making money on a daily basis for authors and publishers without having to cut a distributor in on the profits. This means more money for the author or publisher.

Within most areas of the street market in the northeastern states (NY, NJ, DE, PA, and MD) the average novel is sold or distributed at $10. The price of non-fiction books may vary because these titles are usually more expensive than novels. In the Midwest, southern states and the west coast most novels are sold for full retail price, and nonfiction books in most cases are priced at 80%-100% of the retail price.

Pack your books and hit the subway, train stations, bus stops and areas where there are mass numbers of people congregated in outside areas.

Take the time to visit shopping areas as well. And in some cases you may be able to set up a table with your books and sell them this way.

If you drive then pack your books in your car and hit the road. Wherever there are shopping centers where a lot of people are back and forth outside provides a great opportunity for sales. Finding a few locations where you can set up depends on your time schedule. It may take a few days to a few weeks to begin to see sales, so don't be so quick to become discouraged. Once you sell a few hundred to five hundred copies in an area then move to somewhere else and do the same thing. Take a good percentage of your earnings and reinvest it back into reprinting to keep the cycle going.

Seek to spread out and expand the areas you reach. When you have the opportunity, develop a business relationship with a few vendors who sell books or other items to add your title(s) to their inventory.

The nightlife, club scene, and lounges provide another avenue to garnish book sales. You may be able to link up with a club promoter so you can set up your books at the clubs or venues they promote at.

Utilize your imagination! Wherever there are people there are a percentage who are book readers.

10. Business Credit

Somewhere down the line in order to advance your business you will need business financing. It is always smart to utilize your business credit as opposed to your own personal credit when seeking to obtain business loans. The first step you will need is to incorporate (LLC, S Corp, or other form of corporation) to effectively build a business credit rating.

Business credit is different than personal credit and exists solely based on the business credit worthiness and therefore puts the owners less at risk.

The following companies assist businesses with establishing credit:

Business Builder Enterprises

www.access-business-credit.com
1-800-508-6148

B2BCredit
www.B2Bcredit.com
1-877-464-3700

Dun & Bradstreet
www.dnb.com

Do an online search and check around because there are several business builder companies which provide many different services and programs.
I wish you much success in all your endeavors!

11. True or False

1. Business credit is the same as Personal credit.
   (true) or (false)

2. You should contact Consumer Affairs to obtain information for a copyright.
   (true) or (false)

3. Marketing is not the same as Publicity.
   (true) or (false)

4. ISBN stands for international serial book number.
   (true) or (false)

5. Inbound marketing is a form of advertising.
   (true) or (false)

6. Publicity is about communicating information to the media in order to capture a larger audience.
   (true) or (false)

7. You do not need an ISBN to have your book stocked in stores.
   (true) or (false)

8. Book signings are technically meant for promotional purposes.
   (true) or (false)

9. Book signings normally should not be set up less than six weeks in advance.
   (true) or (false)

10. Street signings are a good example of guerilla marketing.
    (true) or (false)

12. The Path to Success with Ebook and Print Publishing

It's amazing how technology has advanced so much that even the book publishing world has been forced to accept the idea of a book as no longer just being a bound paperback or hardcover. Ebook sales have risen to represent 10% of overall book sales, and the world of publishing has forever changed.

With companies like amazon, bookbaby, smashwords and many others, authors and indie publishers can publish their works as ebooks and distribute them for a fraction of the cost it would take to publish a paperback.

Although authors and indie publishers are basically given an easy lay up with the ebook option, as cost effective as it is the truth still remains, the business of publishing a book and garnishing sales relies heavily on marketing and publicity. If no one knows about your work then they won't purchase it, it's this simple. Authors/Companies must still spend funds to market their names, titles and companies to ensure the title becomes successful.

When aspiring authors, and authors ask me what do I think of ebooks, I always state that an ebook program should be an addition to publishing a physical book for independent authors/publishers. I see it as another avenue to granish sales, not as an escape route for those who don't want to learn the business of publishing a traditional book. Ebooks still only make up 10% of overall book sales, so I don't see it as a viable money making route to avoid paperback or hardcover publishing.

Whether publishing an ebook, audio book, paperback or hardcover, it cannot be stressed enough that writing is 10% inspiration and 90% business. Many happy book sales to all of you.

Therone Shellman is available for interviews and speaking engagements. Please send an email to the below address for inquiries.
theronesbookconsult@yahoo.com

Advertising

KEITH KAREEM WILLIAMS "I Bleed Ink and Write or Die Is My Lifestyle."

SYNOPSIS: Water Flows Under Doors is a gritty urban tale that tells the story of a young man who believes he has lost his woman to another man when in fact, he has lost her to *herself.* To cure his addiction for this woman he becomes addicted to another and just like a new drug, this high is more potent than the last. However, what he's found in this new woman may cost him his life as well as hers.

SYNOPSIS: Enter the world of Mika & Sedari, almost the perfect couple. Their love & devotion is complete except for the open spaces they

71

have allowed to develop in their hearts. When Sedari's dangerous friendships & Mika's deadly past collide, destructive forces are unleashed that shake their marriage to its very foundations. Can they close their open spaces before being pulled so far apart that they may never find their way back to each other? Their marriage stands on the edge of the abyss. Can they stop the events that have been set in motion before blood is spilled and lives are lost? Open Spaces is powerful, entertaining, & honest fiction at its finest.

Follow @ReemtheGullyGod on Twitter

http://thegullygodchronicles.blogspot.com

Both novels are available on amazon.com in paperback and kindle edition

http://www.theroneshellmanskincare.net

Look   For   the   **Therone ShellmanSkincare is coming real soon**

theronesskincare@yahoo.com

THE SUCCESSFUL RISE of ARC BOOK CLUB INC.

"OPENING A WORLD OF LITERARY COMMUNICATION"

ARC Book Club Inc. is a diverse and informative outlet for literary passions. We encourage and support the literary bond between readers and authors. ARC Book Club motivates readers to review literature of both established and debut authors.

Avid Reading Consultants, widely known as ARC, is proud to be one of New York's popular book clubs. Much of ARC's success is attributed to its core standards. Slander is forbidden, and there are guidelines for review writing. Each member has specific duties for which they are held accountable, and it is understood that each individual is a reflection of ARC. Keeping the lines of communication open, staying abreast of literary trends and keeping organizational goals in the forefront of the member's minds has allowed ARC to remain vanguards in the world of book clubs.

ARC Book Club Inc has five members, three of which are reviewers. ARC Reviewers are also sought after by popular authors for their opinions on manuscripts, synopsis writing, book release hosting, editing, and promotional support. Physical and online meetings are conducted monthly for ARC members.

DID YOU KNOW?

Authors across the Waters 2010: In conjunction with London England's Colourful Radio, ARC exposes one American author each month to British readers. Authors are interviewed by presenter Julie Ann Ryan on her radio show.)

ARC partnership with Universal Write Publication (UWP): To promote literacy and education among our youth ARC has collaborated with UWP, a premier educational publisher.   (9/2010)

To request membership
: Sistartea@arcbookclubinc.com